We Need Veterinarians

by Lola M. Schaefer

Consulting Editor: Gail Saunders-Smith, Ph.D.

Consultant: Daniel Simpson, DVM,
West Bay Animal Hospital, Warwick, Rhode Island

Pebble Books

an imprint of Capstone Press
Mankato, Minnesota

Pebble Books are published by Capstone Press
1710 Roe Crest Drive, North Mankato, Minnesota 56003
www.capstonepub.com

Library of Congress Cataloging-in-Publication Data
Schaefer, Lola M., 1950–
    We need veterinarians / by Lola M. Schaefer.
    p. cm.—(Helpers in our community)
    Includes bibliographical references and index.
    Summary: Simple text and photographs present veterinarians and their role in
the community.
    ISBN-13: 978-0-7368-0395-3 (hardcover)   ISBN-10: 0-7368-0395-5 (hardcover)
    ISBN-13: 978-0-7368-4832-9 (pbk.)   ISBN-10: 0-7368-4832-0 (pbk.)
    1. Veterinary medicine—Juvenile literature. 2. Veterinarians—Juvenile
literature. [1. Veterinarians. 2. Occupations.] I. Title. II. Series: Schaefer, Lola M.,
1950- Helpers in our community.
    SF756.S32 2000
    636.089′09′2—dc21   99-19409

Note to Parents and Teachers

The Helpers in Our Community series supports national social
studies standards for units related to community helpers and
their roles. This book describes and illustrates veterinarians and
how they help people care for their animals. The photographs
support early readers in understanding the text. The repetition of
words and phrases helps early readers learn new words. This
book also introduces early readers to subject-specific vocabulary
words, which are defined in the Words to Know section. Early
readers may need assistance to read some words and to use the
Table of Contents, Words to Know, Read More, Internet Sites, and
Index/Word List sections of the book.

Printed in the United States of America in North Mankato, Minnesota.
062013
007377R

Table of Contents

Veterinarians are doctors who care for animals.

Some veterinarians care
for pets.

Some veterinarians care
for farm animals.

Some veterinarians care for zoo animals.

Veterinarians give checkups to animals.

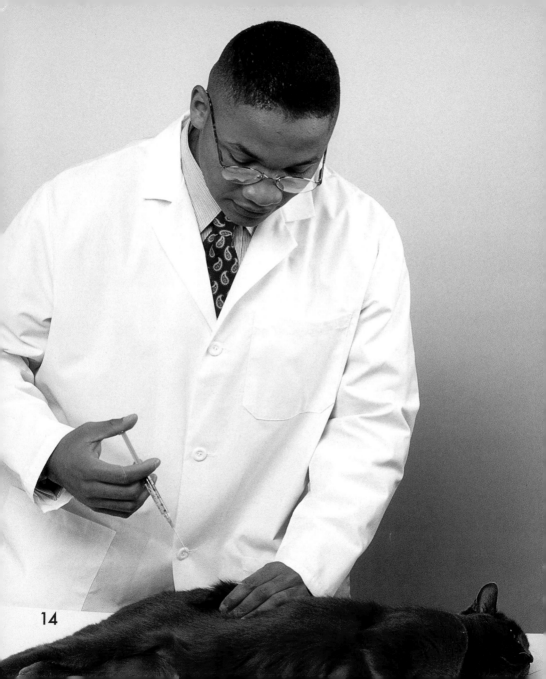

Veterinarians give
medicine to animals.

Veterinarians set
broken bones.

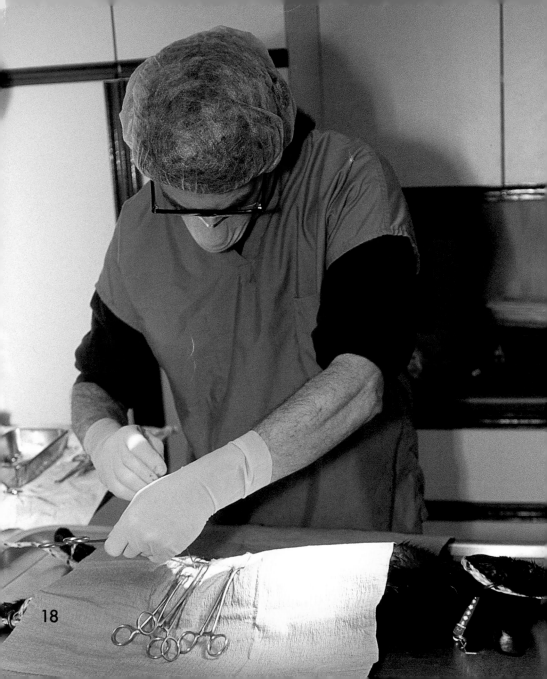

Veterinarians perform surgery on animals.

Veterinarians help keep animals healthy.

Words to Know

doctor—someone trained and licensed to give medical treatment; a veterinarian is trained and licensed to treat animals.

healthy—fit and well; not sick.

medicine—a drug or substance used to treat an illness; veterinarians give medicine to sick animals.

surgery—removing or repairing body parts that are sick or hurt

Read More

Greene, Carol. *Veterinarians Help Animals.* Plymouth, Minn.: Child's World, 1997.

Kunhardt, Edith. *I'm Going to Be a Vet.* Read with Me Paperbacks. New York: Scholastic Press, 1996.

Ready, Dee. *Veterinarians.* Community Helpers. Mankato, Minn.: Bridgestone Books, 1997.

Internet Sites

FactHound offers a safe, fun way to find Internet sites related to this book. All of the sites on FactHound have been researched by our staff.

Here's all you do:

Visit *www.facthound.com*

FactHound will fetch the best sites for you!

Index/Word List

animals, 5, 9, 11, 13, 15, 19, 21
bones, 17
broken, 17
care, 5, 7, 9, 11
checkups, 13
doctors, 5
farm, 9
give, 13, 15
healthy, 21
help, 21
keep, 21
medicine, 15
perform, 19
pets, 7
set, 17
some, 7, 9, 11
surgery, 19
veterinarians, 5, 7, 9, 11, 13, 15, 17, 19, 21
zoo, 11

Word Count: 48
Early-Intervention Level: 9

Editorial Credits
Karen L. Daas, editor; Abby Bradford, Bradfordesign, Inc., cover designer; Kimberly Danger, photo researcher

Photo Credits
David F. Clobes, 8, 10, 16
International Stock/Hal Hern, 1
Kent and Donna Dannen, 12
Photo Network/Andrea Esty, 4; Esbin-Anderson, 14; Phyllis Picardi, 18
Rainbow/Dan McCoy, cover
Stephen Simpson/FPG International LLC, 20
Unicorn Stock Photos/Jim Shippee, 6

24